PAST IN PICTURES

A photographic view of
Home Life

Published in paperback in 2014 by Wayland
Copyright © Wayland 2014

Wayland
338 Euston Road
London NW1 3BH

Wayland Australia
Level 17/207 Kent Street
Sydney, NSW 2000

Editor: Joyce Bentley
Concept Design: Lisa Peacock
Designer: Elaine Wilkinson
Researchers: Laura Simpson and Hester Vaizey at
The National Archives

Picture acknowledgements:
Material reproduced by courtesy of The National Archives, London, England. www.nationalarchives.gov.uk. Catalogue references and picture acknowledgements Main cover: COPY1-565 (81) Maid on telephone 1912 (tl); COAL80-2062 (58) Miners children playing on new housing estate, Cotgrave Notts, 1964 (tr); COPY1-177 (7) Norman & Stacey Ltd Bedroom furniture 1901 (bl); COPY1-439 (451) Laundry maid 1899 (br); Back cover: COPY1-136 (392) Greenwood's Chimney Cleaner 1897 (l); COPY1-420 Vegetable gardening near Chanctonbury Ring, West Sussex, 1895 (r); title page: INF2-44 (2749) Gas cooker in post-war kitchen, 1945; p3: COAL80-2062 (13) Miner with wife and children outside home, Housing and Living conditions, South Wales 1935; p4: COPY1-39 Bedford Park Estate, Turnham Green, London. Plans and Elevations (1), 1877; p5: ZPER34-78 p133 Dinner for the poor at Conder Street Mission Hall, Limehouse 1879; p6: COPY1-420 Vegetable gardening near Chanctonbury Ring, West Sussex, 1895; p7:COPY1-136 (392) Greenwood's Chimney Cleaner 1897; p8: COPY1-439 (451) Laundry maid 1899; p9: Time & Life Pictures/Getty Images; p10: COPY1-169 (223) Bathroom shower attachment 1900; p11: COPY1-177 (7) Norman & Stacey Ltd Bedroom furniture 1901; p12: COPY1-454 Servant washing dishes at a sink with anti-splash tap fitted 1902; p13: COPY1-491 (122) Outdoor washing of laundry 1905; p14: COPY1-492 (4) Children playing in the snow Devon 1905; p15: COPY1-227A (37) Lasso Hand Cleaner, Edward Cook and Co, London, 1905; p16: COAL13 (92) Dinner time 1907-1914_low; p17: COAL80-2062 (31) Housing & living conditions 1910; p18: COPY1-565 (81) Maid on telephone 1912, p19: Hulton-Deutsch Collection/Corbis; p20: COAL80-2062 (13) Miner with wife and children outside home, Housing and Living conditions, South Wales 1935; p21: COAL80-2062 (22) Miner outside home shaking the dirt off his Pit clothes, Housing and Living conditions 1935; p22: INF13-288 (24) If you are bombed out ask to find your rest centre poster; p23: HO186-2247 Ministry of Home Security Baby's Gas Helmet instructions WORLD WAR II GAS ATTACK; p24: INF2-44 (2749) Gas cooker in post-war kitchen, 1945; p25: WORK25-209 Living room on the Poplar Estate, London 1951; p26: WORK25-210 Show House at Annabel Close on the Poplar Estate, London 1951; p27: COAL80-2062 (58) Miners children playing on new housing estate, Cotgrave Notts, 1964; p28: COAL80-2063 (104) First house occupied by transferee in new houses built at Goodyers End Estate, Bedford, Warwickshire 1965; p29: COAL80-2062 (27) Housing & living conditions 1970.

A cataloguing record for this title is available at the British Library.
Dewey number: 941'.082-dc23

ISBN: 978 0 7502 8347 2
Printed in China
10 9 8 7 6 5 4 3 2 1

Wayland is a division of Hachette Children's Books, an Hachette UK company
www.hachette.co.uk

Contents

Introduction

In this book we look at photographs and other kinds of images of homes, from Victorian times up until the 1970s. We examine these images for clues about the past and see what we can learn from them about the way people used to live. On pages 30-31, you can find some questions and points to explore, to encourage further discussion of the pictures.

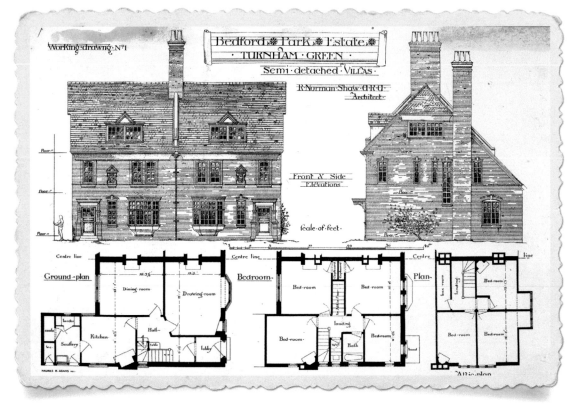

← This is a plan of a 19th century house.

↑ In this plan, we can see an architect's drawing of a house from the front and side. The plans beneath show the layout of the rooms on three floors of the house. Some of the names of the rooms, such as 'scullery' and 'drawing room', are rarely heard today.

1879

⬇ **Some people did not live in a family home.**

↑ Orphans and very poor children often ended up in homes run by charities. This drawing shows children being given a dinner of Irish stew at a home for the poor in Limehouse, London.

1895

⬇ Families often grew their own vegetables.

⬆ Before the 1900s there were no fridges, and food was hardly ever shipped long distances. As a result, people with gardens usually had a vegetable patch to supply them with fresh food. Popular vegetables included potatoes, beans, tomatoes, cucumbers and lettuce.

→ This is an advert for a chimney cleaner.

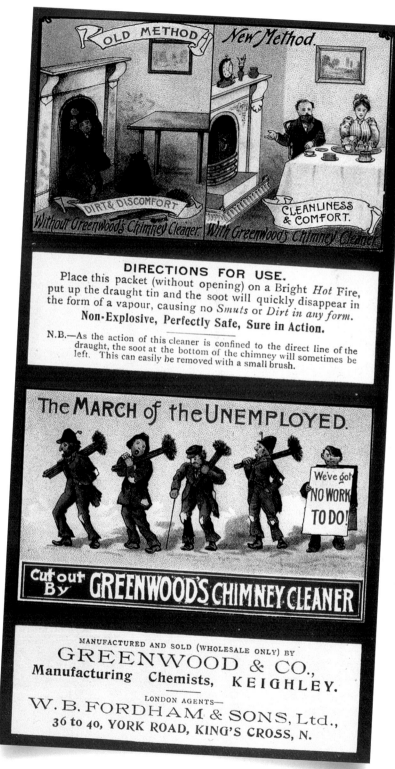

→ Soot from coal fires stained furnishings, carpets, walls and clothing, and was a real problem for Victorian households. This product claims to clean chimneys automatically. You place the packet on a fire and, so it says, 'the soot will quickly disappear'.

← Many families employed maids to help with the housework.

← During the Victorian era, most households employed at least one domestic servant. Poorer families might have a single maid-of-all-work. Rich households kept a number of servants, ranging from a lowly scullery maid to a butler and a housekeeper.

↓ This maid is ironing clothes on a table.

↑ Early irons were heated by being placed near a fire. Some had hot charcoal inside them. The most popular iron at the beginning of the 20th century was the flat iron, shown here. The folding ironing board was invented in the 1860s, but most people continued to use tables, as this woman is doing here.

→ This man is demonstrating how to work a shower.

↑ This early model of a shower worked by filling up a bucket of water from the tap, then releasing the water through holes in the bottom of the bucket by pulling a chain. In 1900, most houses did not even have a bathroom, so any sort of shower would have seemed like the height of luxury!

1901

↓ This is an advertisement for bedroom furniture.

↑ The size of the room and the quality of the furniture suggest that this is a bedroom in a fairly wealthy home. Note the heavily patterned wallpaper and curtains. Darker colours and patterns were more practical because coal fires and gas lighting left stains.

← A servant washes dishes in a sink.

← Sinks only had one tap, providing cold water. Hot water was obtained by heating cold water over a fire. Wealthier homes had indoor plumbing, but many poorer people had to draw their water from pumps in the street.

↓ **Washing clothes was hard work.**

↑ Clothes were washed by hand in the scullery or outside. The woman on the left is heating water in a 'copper' over a fire. The woman on the right is using a washboard – a wood or metal board with grooves cut into it – to scrub the dirt out of the clothes.

↓ These children are playing in the snow.

↑ This picture was used on a Christmas card. It shows wealthy children playing in their garden. Not many families had gardens big enough to play in, and there were no children's playgrounds. Poor children played in the street or the fields, or wherever they could find space.

↓ This is an advert for a hand cleaner.

↑ In the early 1900s, millions of people were employed as domestic servants and tradespeople. Many had to carry out dirty jobs, and there was certainly a need for hand cleaners like this one. The images in this advert give an idea of the people this product was aimed at.

↓ A coalminer has tea with his daughter.

↑ High tea, or meat tea, was the traditional evening meal of working class families, often eaten between 5 and 7pm, when labourers or miners came home from work. It usually included a hot dish, such as fish and chips, followed by tea with cakes and bread, butter and jam.

⇩ This is a mining village in South Wales.

↑ Houses built for miners and factory workers were often cramped and had poor sanitation. They were built close to the local mine or factory and, because everyone worked at the same place, there was usually a strong sense of community.

← A maid is speaking on an intercom.

← An intercom is a device that allows communication within a building. It was invented in 1894. Large houses with several floors used intercoms. The panel above the maid's head contains a light or bell for each room. A light flashes or a bell rings to indicate the room from which the call is being made.

↓ A couple listen to an early type of radio.

↑ In the 1920s, the radio became a popular feature in many homes. Because they were very expensive, many people built their own sets, called crystal radios. The sound they produced was too low to be heard through a speaker, so headphones were used. The British Broadcasting Corporation (BBC) began its first radio broadcasts in November 1922.

↓ **A man greets his wife and children on his return from work.**

↑ Until the 1920s, most people lived in rented housing. Millions of 'two-up, two-down' terraced houses were built to house working class families. They had two main rooms on the ground floor and two bedrooms on the top floor.

↓ A coal miner shakes the dirt off his clothes.

↑ Soot could stain interior furnishings, so miners usually cleaned themselves up a little before entering the house. Cleaning a house was hard physical work. Few people owned vacuum cleaners, and furniture and floors had to be dusted, scrubbed and polished to keep them clean.

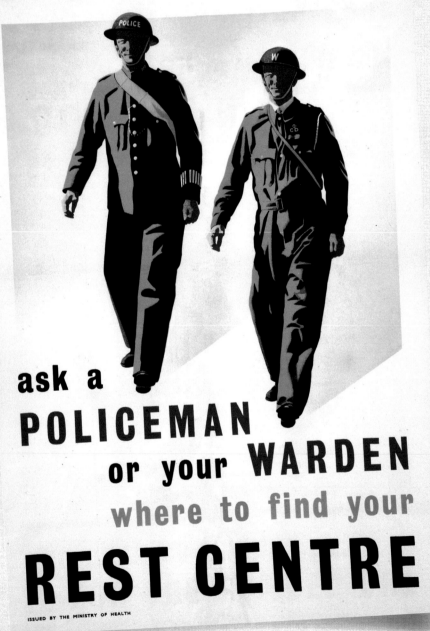

IF YOU ARE BOMBED OUT
and have no friends to go to

ask a
POLICEMAN
or your WARDEN
where to find your
REST CENTRE

ISSUED BY THE MINISTRY OF HEALTH

← During the Second World War, many people's homes were bombed.

← Between September 1940 and May 1941, German bombers launched major raids on British cities during a period known as the Blitz. Thousands of people were killed and more than a million homes were destroyed, leaving countless people homeless. Rest centres quickly filled up, and many depended on friends or relatives for shelter.

➜ This leaflet explains how to put on a baby's gas helmet.

➜ During World War II, the government feared that Britain would be hit by gas bombs. Everyone in the country was sent a gas mask. The black rubber masks were hot, smelly and hard to breathe through. When you breathed in, the air was sucked through a filter to take out the gas. As you can see here, babies were issued with gas helmets rather than masks. Fortunately, Britain never suffered a gas attack.

OFFICIAL INSTRUCTIONS ISSUED BY THE MINISTRY OF HOME SECURITY

What to do about GAS

HINTS TO MOTHERS

★ Learn to put on baby's gas helmet quickly, while wearing your own mask. Your Health Visitor will show you how. If you don't know her address ask at Town Hall or at the Child Welfare Centre.

★ With more than one baby you need help. Arrange with a neighbour, or find out if your local W.V.S. has a Housewives' Service.

★ Toddlers soon learn to put on their own masks. Let them make a game of it and they will wear their gas masks happily.

In a gas attack, first put on your own mask, then you will be better able to help baby.

MAKE SURE YOUR FAMILY HAVE THEIR GAS MASKS WITH THEM NIGHT & DAY

1945

↓ This woman is preparing a meal using an electric cooker.

↑ Electric cookers with ovens and stoves became popular in the late 1920s, when electricity began to be commonly supplied to households. Before that, people used cast-iron ranges heated by coal fires. Electric cookers were popular because the temperature could be controlled, and the enamel surfaces were easy to clean.

↓ **A man relaxes in his living room.**

↑ The living room was the place where people relaxed in the evenings. Here, they read, talked and watched television. Sometimes, as in this case, it doubled as a dining room. In the 1950s most homes did not have central heating, and were heated using gas, electric or traditional coal fires.

↓ **These houses have just been built.**

↑ During the 1950s, many council houses were built. These were cheap homes, built and managed by local councils, mainly for working class families. This is a newly built council estate (housing development) in Poplar, East London.

↓ These children are playing outside their house.

↑ This is a brand-new housing estate in Nottinghamshire. The road is a quiet cul-de-sac, with little traffic. Children from different families mingle freely, and can play on the wide grass verge.

1965

↓ This is a newly built house. The family has just moved in.

↑ Home life in the 1960s was quite different from today. There were no computers, and the TV had just three channels. Married women usually didn't work and did most of the household chores. Meals were mostly cooked and eaten at home – there were very few takeaway restaurants.

⬇ **These are semi-detached houses.**

↑ Semi-detached houses are pairs of houses built side by side as units sharing a wall. The paired houses are usually mirror images of each other. Many semi-detached houses were built in suburbs (areas on the edge of cities) in the 1920s and 1930s. They were popular with middle class families.

Questions to Ask and Points to Explore

Picture on page 4

Questions to ask

1. This is a drawing of a house that has not yet been built. Why does the architect need to draw a plan? Who will look at this? Why would they want to see the front and the side of the house?

2. What is a scullery?

3. How were drawing rooms used?

4. How many bedrooms will there be?

Points to explore

Drawing: style, purpose

Building: purpose; what sort of people would live here?

Picture on page 5

Questions to ask

1. What do you think the girl on the right is asking for?

2. Why do you think some children are eating standing up?

Points to explore

Drawing: style, purpose

Room: furniture, utensils, crowdedness

People: clothing, ages, expressions

Photograph on page 6

Questions to ask

1. Can you see what sort of vegetable is being grown here?

2. What time of year do you think this is, and why?

3. What type of house do these people live in?

Points to explore

Background: building, materials, state of repair

People: gender, ages, clothes

Picture on page 7

Questions to ask

1. At the top of the advert, the two pictures show a room before and after using this product. Do you think this sort of advert would have been effective?

2. The lower picture shows a line of men carrying brushes. One of them is carrying a sign saying 'We've got no work to do!'.

Can you work out who these men are supposed to be and why they have no work?

Points to explore

Drawing: style, purpose

People: clothing, job

Photograph on page 8

Questions to ask

1. This is a laundry maid. What do you think she is carrying?

2. Why do you think a family employed a maid to do the laundry? How was laundry work different from today?

Points to explore

Background: building, materials

Person: gender, age, clothes, expression

Photograph on page 9

Questions to ask

1. Why is the maid ironing near the fireplace?

2. Why do you think she's standing close to the window?

Points to explore

Background: furniture, fireplace, clock, window, floor

Person: gender, age, clothing

Picture on page 10

Questions to ask

1. Can you see how this shower would have worked?

2. Most houses did not have a bathroom in 1900. How did people keep themselves clean?

Points to explore

Drawing: style, purpose

Content: style of bath, tiling, clothing

Picture on page 11

Questions to ask

1. Why is there a fireplace in the bedroom?

2. Can you guess what the jugs and bowls on the cabinet surface, and the towels next to them, are for?

Points to explore

Drawing: style, purpose

Conent: wallpaper and curtains, furniture design

Photograph on page 12

Questions to ask

1. Why is there a metal plate fixed to the wall behind the sink?

2. It looks like a carpet on the floor. Do you think that would have been a practical sort of floor covering for this room?

Points to explore

Background: sink and tap design, flooring

Person: gender, age, uniform

Photograph on page 13

Questions to ask

1. Why do you think the laundry was often done outside?

2. Washing machines were available by this time, though they were not widespread, and by 1914 were only found in about 5 per cent of homes. Why do think this was?

Points to explore

Background: garden, equipment, dog

People: gender, clothing, age, pose

Photograph on page 14

Questions to ask

1. Can you see what the children are doing?

2. The girl in the centre is carrying a fur tube for keeping her hands warm. Do you know what this is called?

Points to explore

Background: path, weather, time of year

People: age, clothing, umbrella

Photograph on page 15

Questions to ask

1. Can you work out the jobs of the people shown in this picture?

2. Why would they need a hand cleaner?

Points to explore

Advert: style, purpose

People: clothing, gender, jobs

Photograph on page 16

Questions to ask

1. Why do you think the man has a dirty face and clothes?

2. The furnishings and tableware in this

photograph look very fine and well cared for, yet coalminers do not earn much money. What does this tell us about the family?

Points to explore

Background: curtains, tablecloth, crockery, wallpaper, cake

People: age, expressions, clothing

Photograph on page 17

Questions to ask

1. Why do you think people are standing on their front doorsteps?

2. The front of some of the houses looks quite sooty. Why do you think that is?

Points to explore

Background: building style, materials and quality

People: gender, clothing, pose

Photograph on page 18

Questions to ask

1. Why were intercom systems installed?

2. The intercom device that the maid is holding is similar to an old-fashioned telephone. Can you guess what she must speak into in order to reply?

Points to explore

Background: equipment function and design

Person: gender, age, uniform, hairstyle

Photograph on page 19

Questions to ask

1. Why are the couple listening through headphones?

2. How does this living room differ from most modern living rooms? Do you think tastes have changed since the 1920s?

Points to explore

Background: wallpaper, fireplace, tablecloth, pictures, mantelpiece ornaments, book, newspaper, cat

Person: clothing, age, expressions

Photograph on page 20

Questions to ask

1. Why is this woman wearing an apron?

2. Why is her husband wearing a suit and tie?

Points to explore

Background: building, materials, quality

People: clothing, cap, ages, gender, expressions

Photograph on page 21

Questions to ask

1. Why is this man dirty?

2. Why is he outside his house?

Points to explore

Background: building, materials, cleanliness

Person: clothing, dirt, gender

Picture on page 22

Questions to ask

1. Why do you think this poster was needed, and do you think it does a good job of telling people what they need to know?

2. Who were wardens, also known as ARP wardens, and what was their job? Why did they wear tin helmets?

Points to explore

Poster: design, typography, style of illustration

People: gender, uniform

Photograph on page 23

Questions to ask

1. Why do you think babies were issued with gas helmets rather than gas masks?

2. Do you think this leaflet would have been helpful to mothers? It doesn't explain how to put on a gas helmet, so what advice does it give? Why do you think it was aimed at mothers, not fathers?

Points to explore

Illustration: gender, clothing, gas mask, gas helmet

Text: meaning of terms: Ministry of Home Security; Health Visitor; Town Hall; WVS (Women's Voluntary Service); Housewives' Service

Photograph on page 24

Questions to ask

1. In what ways is this different from a modern cooker?

2. What do you think the shelf on the left of the picture was used for?

3. How easy would it have been to clean this kitchen?

Points to explore

Room: equipment, materials, kitchen design

Person: gender, clothing

Photograph on page 25

Questions to ask

1. Can you see the television. How does it

differ from modern televisions?

2. What is the bucket by the fireplace used for?

Points to explore

Room: heating, lighting, furnishings

Person: clothing, hairstyle, pose

Photograph on page 26

Questions to ask

1. The house at the end of the terrace with the man standing outside it is a show house. Do you know what a show house is?

2. Why do you think there was a need for new housing in London after the Second World War?

Points to explore

Housing: design, materials, attractiveness

Man: uniform

Street: emptiness

Photograph on page 27

Questions to ask

1. Do you think this is a safe environment for children? Why do you think that?

2. How is this similar to and different from a street scene today?

Points to explore

Background: houses, cars, toys

People: ages, clothing, hairstyles

Photograph on page 28

Questions to ask

1. How can you tell that these children have just moved in?

2. How do the furniture and furnishings differ from a modern house?

Points to explore

Rooms: furnishings, carpet, television, fireplace

People: ages, clothing

Photograph on page 29

Questions to ask

1. Why do you think the houses have been set back from the main road?

2. Why was an area with grass and trees placed near the houses?

3. Can you think of anything that is different about these houses compared to modern houses?

Points to explore

Background: house design and materials, road, green area

Some suggested answers can be found on the Wayland website www.waylandbooks.co.uk.

Further Information

Books

Home Life *(Britain Since 1948)* by Neil Tonge (Wayland, 2008)
Home Life *(Britain Since World War II)* by Stewart Ross (Franklin Watts, 2007)
Home Life in the 1930s and 40s *(When I Was Young)* by Faye Gardner (Evans Brothers, 2011)
Victorian Homes *(Life in the Past)* by Mandy Ross (Heinemann Library, 2004)

Websites

http://www.bbc.co.uk/schools/primaryhistory/world_war2/daily_life/
http://www.bbc.co.uk/schools/primaryhistory/world_war2/wartime_homes/
http://www.chiddingstone.kent.sch.uk/homework/houses/victorian.htm
http://www.1900s.org.uk

Glossary

architect A person who designs buildings.

butler The chief male servant of a household.

charity An organisation set up to provide help for those in need.

cul-de-sac A street that is closed at one end.

domestic Relating to home life.

drawing room A room in a large, private house in which guests can be received and entertained.

gas lighting Lighting produced by burning gas – this was the main form of lighting in the 1800s, before the arrival of electric lighting.

housekeeper A woman employed to manage a household.

housing estate A residential area in which the houses have all been planned and built at the same time.

layout The way in which the parts of something are arranged or laid out.

maid-of-all-work A maid employed as the only servant in poorer households.

middle class The social group between the upper and working classes, including professional workers and their families.

nursery A room in a house for the special use of young children.

plumbing The system of pipes, tanks, fittings and other equipment required to supply water, heating and sanitation to a building.

sanitation The provision of clean drinking water and adequate sewage disposal.

scullery A small room at the back of a house used for washing dishes, clothing and other household work.

semi-detached house A house joined to another house on one side by a shared wall.

suburb A residential area (i.e. an area where people live) that is located close to a city.

terraced houses A row of houses that are joined to each other by shared walls.

working class The social group made up of people who do manual or industrial work, and their families.